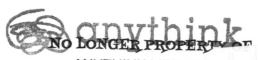

HORSES

EZ READERS

Miriam Z.

Creating Young Nonfiction Readers

EZ Readers lets children delve into nonfiction at beginning reading levels. Young readers are introduced to new concepts, facts, ideas, and vocabulary.

Tips for Reading Nonfiction with Beginning Readers

Talk about Nonfiction
Begin by explaining that nonfiction books give us information that is true. The book will be organized around a specific topic or idea, and we may learn new facts through reading.

Look at the Parts
Most nonfiction books have helpful features. Our *EZ Readers* include a Table of Contents, an index, a picture glossary and color photographs. Share the purpose of these features with your reader.

Table of Contents
Located at the front of a book, the Table of Contents displays a list of the big ideas within the book and where to find them.

Index
An index is an alphabetical list of topics and the page numbers where they are found.

Picture Glossary
Located at the back of the book, a picture glossary contains key words/phrases that are related to the topic.

Photos/Charts
A lot of information can be found by "reading" the charts and photos found within nonfiction text. Help your reader learn more about the different ways information can be displayed.

With a little help and guidance about reading nonfiction, you can feel good about introducing a young reader to the world of *EZ Readers* nonfiction books.

Printing 1 2 3 4 5 6 7 8 9

Author: Miriam Z.
Designer: Cornell Whitehead
Editor: Editorial Staff

Names/credits:
Title: Horses / by Miriam Z.
Description: Hallandale, FL : Mitchell Lane Publishers, [2018]

Series: Pets Books

Library bound ISBN: 9781680202052

eBook ISBN: 9781680202069

EZ readers is an imprint of Mitchell Lane Publishers

Photo credits: Getty Images

Table of Contents

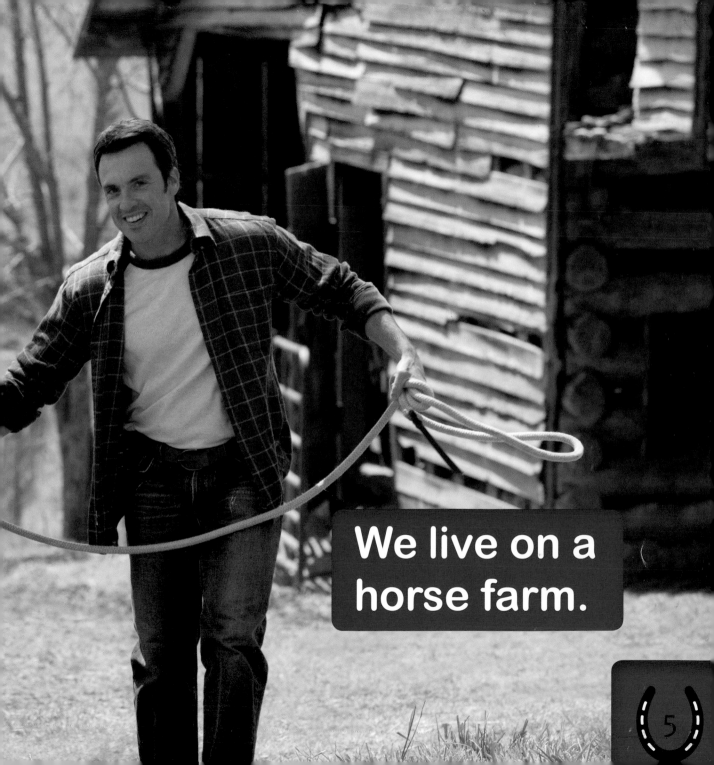

We live on a
horse farm.

5

We have
many horses.

7

Our horses like
to walk on grass.

8

9

They like to trot.

They like to jump.

Some horses race.

15

They eat grass.

17

They like apples, too.

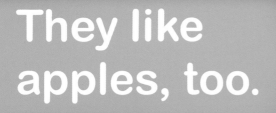

We love
our horses.

20

21

Parts of a Horse

Eyes
A horse's eyes are set on the side ot its head so it can see forwards and backwards.

Ears
Horses have excellent hearing. Their ears rotate to hear sounds in all directions.

Tail
The tail is used to express mood, balancing, and swishing away insects.

Face
The face and head are the most sensitive of a horse's body parts.

Muzzle
A horse's muzzle includes the mouth, nostrils, chin, lips and front of the nose.

Hoof
The hoof is a very important body part. It is comparable to our fingernails.

Whiskers
Whiskers help the horse sense things close to its nose.

Picture Glossary

apples

A round fruit with red, yellow, or green skin and white flesh.

race

A competition between animals to see which one is the fastest.

farm

A piece of land used for growing crops or raising animals.

trot

How a horse moves that is faster than walking.

grass

Plants with green leaves, that are eaten by cows, sheep, horses, etc.

walk

To move with your legs at a speed that is slower than running.

jump

To move the body upward from the ground through the air.

Index